Karen,

In your spare time I thought you could create some great looking bears! Have fun.

Love,
Georger

MAKING
TEDDY BEARS

MAKING
TEDDY BEARS

Jennie Kants

Bloomsbury Books
London

Previous page: This is a shaggy bear, the style of which many of us will remember from our childhood. He is about to go for a sail.

Published by Harlaxton Publishing Ltd
2 Avenue Road, Grantham, Lincolnshire, NG31 6TA, United Kingdom.
A member of the Weldon International Group of Companies.

First published in 1994

This edition published in 1994 by
Bloomsbury Books
an imprint of
The Godfrey Cave Group
42 Bloomsbury Street, London. WC1B 3QJ
under license from Harlaxton Publishing Ltd.

Publisher: Robin Burgess
Editor: Dulcie Andrews
Illustrator: Sam Denley
Photographer: James Duncan
Typesetting: Sellers, Grantham
Colour separation: G A Graphics, Stamford
Produced in Singapore by Imago

British Library Cataloguing-in-Publication data.
A catalogue record for this book is available from the British Library.
Title: Country Craft Series: Making Teddy Bears
ISBN: 1-85471-427-9

CONTENTS

INTRODUCTION

Through this Country Craft series, it is our hope that you will find satisfaction and enjoyment in learning a new skill. In this case, that of making a teddy bear.

The creative pleasures of sewing come to the fore in the making of a teddy bear, that childhood cuddly toy which brings a human warmth into our lives. Many people still have the bear that saw them through dark and lonely nights under the bedcovers and, indeed, bears which have been handed down from generation to generation are now sought-after by collectors of antiques. The prices they bring at auction in the capitals of the world are breathtakingly high.

In Chapter One, we introduce you to a little of the teddy bear's history, before devoting the rest of the book to straight-forward advice on the various steps involved in creating bears. The photographs and illustrations in this book explain the creative sewing process in detail. In the Beginner's Project, we show you how to make the bear seen on the cover. The pattern is included and can be used the same size or enlarged.

The bear you make will have its own character; its face will develop with each stitch and you will be surprised at the result. You will have created a friend for life. One that family and friends will love as much as you do. With experience and confidence, you can create a complete bear family.

Opposite: A young bear is taught the skilful game of draughts by its parent. Patience is a bears's first virtue.

GETTING STARTED

IT IS UNDENIABLE that people of all ages love teddy bears. Most of us owned a favourite teddy as a child and, indeed, many of these childhood companions remain with their owners all their lives.

Teddy-bear characters can be found in children's books, cartoons, films and television programmes and the selection of bears available in toy stores and gift shops is bewildering. Teddy bears are popular gifts for people of all ages, often symbolizing friendship or love, and pictures of teddies abound on greetings cards, gift wrap and a multitude of other items. The teddy bear has become such an important part of our culture that most people are surprised when they learn that teddy bears were invented as late as 1903. This faithful friend and companion seems to have always been with us.

Before we begin to learn the craft of teddy-bear making, let us look at the teddy bear's fascinating and somewhat controversial history.

HISTORY

Since early times, the bear featured around the world in folktales, legend and fairy stories, as an endearing and popular hero, but there is some confusion over who actually invented the teddy bear. America and Germany both claim his origin. Americans believe that the first Teddy bear was the result of President Theodore Roosevelt's visit to the southern states of Louisiana and Mississippi, where he was to resolve a border dispute. Theodore Roosevelt (who was nicked-named Teddy) was a keen hunter and particularly loved bear hunting. Unfortunately, there were few bears to be found in the area at the time and the President's hosts felt obliged to produce one. It was a small and helpless-looking specimen that they found, which they tied to a tree outside the President's tent. When Teddy Roosevelt realized the situation and refused to shoot the pathetic creature, a political cartoonist, Clifford Berryman, recorded the scene in the 'Washington Star'.

The President's act of mercy impressed a Brooklyn sweet shop owner, a Russian immigrant, Morris Michton. His wife, who sewed soft toys and dolls, made up a jointed bear which was displayed in the sweet shop window along with Clifford Berryman's cartoon. The bear proved so popular, Mrs. Michton had difficulty keeping up with the orders. (The Michton's, in time, sold their idea to the Ideal Toy Corporation.) They sent a bear to Teddy Roosevelt, requesting that they called the new toy a 'Teddy' Bear. When his permission was granted, America claims the teddy bear was born.

Meanwhile, on the other side of the

Opposite: Paddington Bear is surely the world's most recognizable bear. His adventures keep us amused for hours.

and a student at Giengen's Technical College and would sketch animals for Margarete at Stuttgart Zoo. Richard suggested a toy bear, to be made of fur with a moving head and limbs. The completed bear was exhibited at Leipzig in 1903 along with other Steiff family toys, but it failed to arouse any interest at first. However, on the last day of the fair, an American, looking for something different and novel, noticed the bear. The result was an order for 3,000 similar bears. The American exhibited these bears in New York where they were spotted by the designer who was responsible for decorating the tables at the wedding of the daughter of Theodore Roosevelt. He invested in one of these brown bears, because of the President's love of hunting and bear hunting in particular. During the wedding, the guests joked about the 'Teddy' bear – thus the Germans lay claim to the invention of the teddy bear.

Above: A dark brown, long-haired bear appears to radiate an entirely different attitude because of the placement of his eyes and his nose. His bow tie is another matter.

Arctophiles, as bear enthusiasts are known, (from the Greek arctos, meaning bear) enjoy endless discussions on the origin of the teddy bear, but it is unlikely that they will ever reach a satisfactory conclusion, except to maintain that the true father of the teddy bear was indeed Theodore Roosevelt.

Atlantic, there was a young German girl, Margarete Steiff, who was paralyzed and confined to a wheelchair. Margarete lived in Giengen, the town where the sewing machine was invented and she was determined to make a living for herself by sewing children's clothes. Giengen was also the centre of felt manufacture and she had the idea of making a felt pin cushion in the shape of an elephant. Mothers bought these felt elephants, but gave them to their children to play with and Margarete, with the help of her five nephews, soon became a manufacturer of toys.

One of the nephews, Richard, was a poet

As his popularity grew during this century, the teddy bear became the hero of children's literary classics such as 'Winnie-the-Pooh', 'Rupert Bear' and the 'Paddington' books. When hundreds of British children were evacuated during the Second World War, each child was given a teddy to take with them and the famous Great Ormond Street Hospital for Sick Children in London has a teddy bear as its symbol and gives a special teddy to the babies who spend time there. The teddy bear is now an international star and an enduring symbol of childhood.

Old, well-preserved bears demand high prices at auction, especially the earliest and rarest specimens and, with the resurgence of interest in traditional teddy bears, Steiff and some other bear-making companies are releasing limited editions of some of the earliest of their designs. These 'real' bears are also being made by individuals, known as bear artists.

BEAR ARTISTS

As a pastime, making a teddy bear can be not only satisfying but also lucrative, and many craftspeople and doll-makers have turned their skills to producing teddy bears of all kinds. These are talented people who can demand high prices for their beautiful, hand-made characters. The bear artists are, of course, highly skilled in the sewing techniques required, but they also have the creative flair needed to produce a teddy bear that is unique.

The bear artists will design the bear and sew it by hand or machine (or they may even have a small cottage industry, where they employ others to do the basic construction). Finally, the bear artist will always do the facial stitching that gives each bear its individuality.

GIFT BEARS

Making teddy bears is a relaxing, creative and infinitely rewarding pastime, whether you want to make simple soft toys or to eventually produce work like that of the bear artists. One of the greatest delights of the craft is the pleasure you can give someone – young or old – when you present them with their own, unique, hand-made bear.

Bears make suitable gifts for a multitude of

Opposite: Bears are quite well-read, even bookish, in the privacy of their own homes. Some have thought of appearing on television quiz shows, but modesty prevents them from doing so.

occasions – anniversaries, birthdays, christenings and so on – with the advantage that they can be personalized, dressed up or embroidered with messages to suit the recipient or festivity. They can carry messages in their hands or wear labels or ribbons embroidered with the name, date and occasion.

With a little patience and practice, and with the help of this book, you will find that in no time you are creating delightful and unique teddy bears which could become the family heirlooms of the future. It could even be the beginning of a small business.

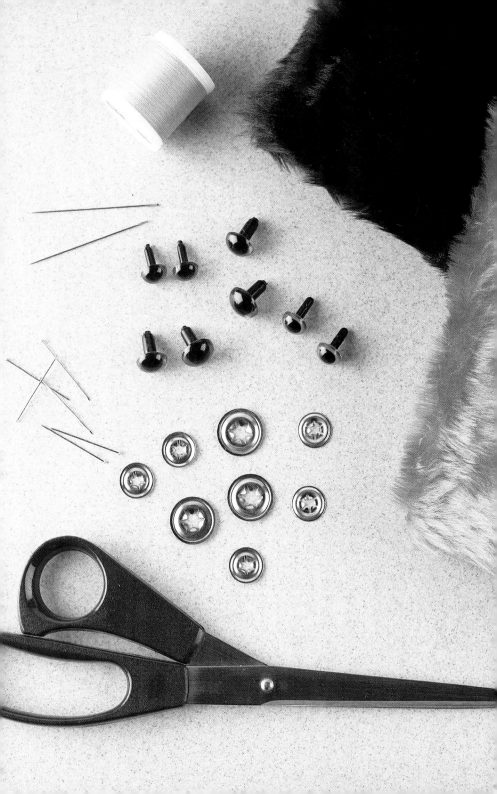

TOOLS AND MATERIALS

HAND-MADE BEARS are expensive to buy; however, in a material sense, a bear can be quite inexpensive to make. In fact, like most hobbies, teddy-bear making can be as costly as you like, depending on the direction you wish to take. An inexpensive bear can be made from bits and pieces picked up from second-hand shops, off-cuts from your own sewing or from an ordinary fabric and haberdashery store. Or, if you wish, you can invest money in expensive fur fabric, such as 'long-pile' mohair and glass eyes. These, and the like, you will find at quality craft suppliers.

ACCESSORIES

You will find a selection of accessories for soft-toy making at good craft and hobby suppliers and in the sewing section of large department stores.

Teddy bear joints

Plastic snap-together joints are used by most manufacturers today and these are available at most craft shops. They are easy to use and are washable. Always invest in good-quality joints as the cheaper ones can come apart. For the 'Beginner's Project' in this book we will use the plastic snap-together joints, but it is possible to make up a set of bear joints yourself from discs (which would have to be made out of plastic, cardboard or plywood) washers and split pins, all available from hard-wear and do-it-yourself stores.

Stuffing material

Polyester filler is light, soft and washable and is available at most craft stores. For convenience, this is the filling we will use for the 'Beginner's Project'. There are, however, any number of fillings that can be used. If you have access to any suitable filling, by all means use it. Wood shavings were used for stuffing the earlier bears; kapok and cotton batting work well, but you must be careful as these stuffings tend to give the bear a lumpy finish. Raw wool is also appropriate. The bear's final appearance will depend on the stuffing you use. Stuffing, like everything else, can take time to master.

Eyes

Glass eyes mounted on wire and 'safety-lock' plastic eyes are the two choices available from the local craft store. The glass eyes are expensive and can break, but are a good choice for a collectable bear, giving an 'alive' quality. It is important to remember that glass eyes should never be used for a child's toy: the 'safety-lock' eyes are a necessity when sewing a teddy bear for a child, particularly for a child under three years of age. Best of all are boot buttons; they give a lovely, soft old-fashioned look. Half-ball black buttons on a metal shank can be bought new in some fabric and haberdashery stores or old ones may be found in second-hand stores. Do not use boot buttons on a child's teddy bear.

Opposite: A collection of items you require to begin making a teddy bear.

Paws, pads and inner ears

Paws, pads and inner ears should usually be cut from a different fabric to the rest of the bear. Colourwise they can be matching or contrasting. Some suggestions of suitable fabrics are: satin, velvet, fine leather, felt, suede or the fluffy side of a good-quality track suit fabric. If using satin, cut the inner ear from the shiny side and the paws and pads from the dull side. This gives an excellent effect of the different texture of the bear's skin. The inner ears can also be cut from the same material as the bear's body.

Nose

For the 'Beginner's Project' in this book, the nose has been embroidered using a six-stranded embroidery cotton (thread) in an appropriate colour. A good way to feminize a bear is to use a soft pink thread for the nose.

Plastic bear noses can be bought from craft suppliers but are not as appealing as the soft, satin-stitched nose.

TOOLS

To make a teddy bear you require very few tools other than those you already have in your sewing basket. There are, however, some optional extras you may wish to invest in.

Scissors

You will require a pair of sharp dress-making scissors. Pointed scissors are a help when cutting fur fabric, but the most important consideration is the sharpness. Keep the dress-making scissors for cutting fabric only – not for craft and kitchen work.

Pins

Strong, extra long pins with glass heads are the best choice. Because you are dealing with thick fabric, you need pins that are longer than ordinary dress-maker's pins.

Needles

Any dressmaker's sewing or machine needles will do, but a heavy duty sewing machine needle is stronger when sewing such thick material. An embroidery needle with a larger eye is easier to thread with the six-stranded cotton (thread), when embroidering the nose. A doll-maker's needle – 7.5cm-20cm (3-8 inches) long – for stitching through the head when attaching the eyes makes the job easier.

Thread

Matching thread is required for the sewing machine and for stitching together the openings for stuffing on the arms and legs. Six-stranded embroidery cotton (thread) is a good, strong thread for stitching on the eyes, ears and head and has the added advantage of coming in a multitude of colours so you can easily match the thread to the cloth.

Stuffing tool

It is difficult to push the stuffing into the ends of the legs and the paws with your fingers and the handle of the wooden spoon makes the perfect tool and can be found in every kitchen. It can also be used to help to turn the limbs inside out. Chop-sticks and blunt knitting needles work well, too, but be careful using anything that is sharp, such as a pair of pointed scissors, as this could cause damage by piercing the fabric.

Thimble

A thimble is a very useful tool when working with stubborn needles in thick fabric.

Teazling brush

A small wire dog brush can be useful for brushing pile out of the seams.

Apron

An apron will keep fluff off your clothes when you are cutting into fur fabric.

Above: Note the shape of the bears' noses. They define their owners' character.

Marking pen

You will need a thick marking pen to mark where the positions for the holes of the joints should be made. You will also require a finer pen to transfer any information which is on the pattern to the wrong side of the fabric when you have cut out the cloth.

Awl

This tool is used to push through the fabric at the 'joint positions' to make a hole, without cutting, for the shank of the joint to be inserted. Cutting a hole with scissors could weaken the fabric.

Glue

Glue is not by any means a necessity, but you may like to stick, as well as stitch, the head to the body.

FABRICS

In the next chapter we will discuss the types of fabric you can use to make bears in many different styles. To begin with, try choosing a fabric that has a short pile as you will find this much easier to sew with than one with long, thick fur.

STARTING WORK

THE DESIGN OR SHAPE of the teddy bear, together with the choice of fabric, are by far the most important decisions to be made. It is here that the task begins.

SHAPES OF TEDDY BEARS

The modern teddy bears have in many ways forgotten their ancestors' origins and have lost a lot of the character they once had. Their proportions have changed dramatically – the teddy bears produced in the early 1900's by the Ideal Toy Corporation (America) and the Steiff Company (Germany) were very different in design from the bears of today. In the early years their bodies were taller, not as round, and with a pronounced hump; their heads were smaller, with a deep long muzzle. Their limbs were longer and thinner. They had the look of a real bear, particularly the Steiff bear (which was designed after a careful study of the real animal).

During the early 1900's Steiff exported many bears to England and, by 1910, many English toy companies were manufacturing their own bears. They originally based their bear design on those imported from Germany, but soon developed their own style. The English bears generally had a bigger head, with a shorter nose; their bodies were plumper and shorter, usually without a hump. Their limbs were shorter and their paws smaller.

The modern teddy bears are now primarily made of acrylic fur fabric and are stuffed with polyester filler. They are cuter, softer looking and are not always jointed. Boot buttons were used for the eyes of the original bears, whereas the eyes of the modern bear are usually of pop-in plastic. This is one of the areas where the modern bear seems to have lost the intelligence and charm it once had. Take a look around your local toy stores and antique toy specialists to get a good idea of the many different designs of teddy bears.

You will find a wide selection of patterns for bears featured in craft and toy-making magazines and specialist books. Your local craft or hobby store is a good place to start looking, followed by a visit to a quality bookstore. Take time to study the various patterns and styles, both traditional and modern, until you find a bear you really like.

When making any form of stuffed toy it is wise to follow the pattern closely. Only deviate from the original pattern when the process becomes more familiar. When you have made up the bear two or three times you may wish to experiment by lengthening the limbs or the nose, or even making the teddy bear fatter. It is in this kind of experimentation that you enter the world of bear artists.

One of the joys of making teddy bears is that they do not have to be perfect; they will

Opposite: A large and floppy bow suits this elegant and rotund bear. The expression on his face is created by the placement of the eyes and the shapes of the nose.

all come out with different expressions. It is, in fact, very difficult exactly to reproduce a bear from a pattern – they seem to take on a life of their own.

FABRIC CHOICES

There are many types of fabric suitable for making teddy bears available today and some of the most popular are discussed below. The length and the thickness of the pile can make a great difference to the overall look of the bear. If it is too short or has no pile at all, like upholstery fabric, the bear will look thin and willowy; if it is too long the bear may look portly and his features could look too small. However, once you begin experimenting, you may very well be looking for just these differences.

Velvet or velveteen, textured wool and corduroy

These fabrics work very well for a 'home-made' look and have the advantage of being inexpensive. Bears made from these would cause no concern to the maker, if they spent a lot of their time being dragged around the floor, put through the washing machine and hung on the clothes line.

Felt

This can be an interesting fabric to use as it has no grain or nap, does not fray and can be stretched a little to mold into shape. The drawback is that it is not washable, but it can be brushed gently or lightly sponged with a damp cloth.

Jersey-backed bear-look fur

This is the fabric used for our 'Beginner's Project' and is readily available at most craft or fabric stores. This is the type of fabric many commercial bears are made of and is relatively inexpensive and easy to care for.

Mohair pile

Mohair pile fabric, made from the long, strong hair of the angora goat, is now made almost exclusively for teddy-bear making and can be well worth the extra expense. It comes in many different colours, lengths and densities and is used to make the best-quality traditional bear.

SOME MORE UNUSUAL CHOICES

If you wish to make a bear that is really different and you are more interested in the teddy bears which are made by bear artists, the possibilities are endless. A few interesting ideas are outlined below.

Patchwork

Crazy patchwork bears can be made either by hand or machine. Special scraps collected over the years can be sewn into your own personal 'memory bear', reminiscent of the old idea of a 'memory quilt'. The more varied the scraps, the richer the look of the bear. Velvet, silk, brocade and satin all go together to create a special and original teddy bear.

Candlewick

Bedspreads and dressing-gowns are traditionally made of this fabric. Candlewick is made from 100 per cent cotton with a long, not very thick pile and, when dyed, gives the bear an immediate look of age. You could almost believe that your new bear has been through the washing machine several times.

To dye your piece of candlewick use hot-water dye. Put the fabric through two separate baths of different colours, one after another, in a pot that is too small for the fabric to move around easily. In between each bath, rinse well. By using a dye pot that is too small, you will get a patchy effect which looks better than an even colour.

Candlewick can be bought from manchester manufacturers or from 'bargain' fabric stores which deal on off-cuts and cheaper lines. Old pieces of candlewick can be picked up at second-hand stores and jumble sales.

Upholstery fabric

This fabric is suitable for making unusual and eye-catching bears. Any non-pile fabric can be used, but a stronger, heavier weight fabric gives a smoother finish when stuffing your bear. If the fabric is too light or stretchy, the finished bear is likely to look lumpy no matter how hard you try to smooth the filling.

Old fur coats

Old fur coats can be picked up very cheaply in second-hand stores, flea markets and garage sales these days and they can be used to make a very special, soft and silky, teddy bear. Make sure that in cutting out this bear you keep the direction of the fur in mind, so the finished result will be a bear with a real flowing look to his fur.

WORK AREA

You do not need a lot of space to begin the craft of teddy-bear making, but it does help if you have a place where you can leave your work out between sessions, with adequate storage for your materials. A comfortable chair and good natural and artificial light will help make teddy-bear making a pleasure eagerly anticipated.

GLOSSARY

There may be some unfamiliar words used throughout this book which are really just basic sewing terms. This list will help you understand their meanings.

Bias – To cut a strip of fabric diagonally across the grain. Bias binding can be cut from the material you are using or it can be bought, to match, from a haberdashery store.

Ease – Extra length to one side of a seam joining two parts of a garment.

Grain – The direction in which the thread runs in a piece of fabric. The threads run both vertically and horizontally (the warp and the weft); to match the grain means to match either of these directions.

Nap – The direction of pile which reflects different lights in each direction. All pieces must be cut with the nap in one direction.

Pile – Fabric woven with sets of looped or cut yarn raised on to one surface. Towelling's pile is looped; velvet's pile is cut.

Selvedge – Finished length-wise edges of a piece of fabric.

Teazling – To brush out fur.

Next page: Having a picnic is what all teddy bear families do as soon as it is warm enough. Honey-filled tarts are always eaten first. Vegetables are not eaten.

TECHNIQUES OF THE CRAFT

THE TECHNIQUES USED for making teddy bears are basically the same as those of a dressmaker.

THE PATTERN

If you choose a pattern from a craft magazine or book, you may find that you need to enlarge the pattern which has been reduced in size to fit the pages of the publication. If so, follow their instructions carefully. The most important part of drawing up a pattern is to keep the curves in the lines.

Using a grid and with a sharp soft pencil, begin drawing at a point where the pattern line coincides with the intersection of four squares. Mark this point where the pattern line intersects with a line of the grid. Join up the marks. Do not use straight lines; but by following the lines with your eye, draw the curves into the pattern lines.

If you choose to use the pattern supplied in this book, you can photocopy the pattern or trace it directly from the pages. Take care that the tracing paper does not move; it is important that the pattern is exact.

Transfer all the information from the printed pattern to each pattern piece such as grain direction and so on. Label all the pieces with the name of the part of the bear (foot pad, outer ear, inner ear, etc.). Cut out all the pieces carefully and mark all joint positions with a marking pen.

If you wish to keep the bear pattern for further use, cut a new set out of a thick non-iron interfacing. This pattern will last time and time again.

CUTTING OUT

The secret of successful sewing lies in really good cutting. Pin out the pattern with care and take your time to cut out the pieces.

Always pin pattern pieces to the wrong side of the fabric, then you can mark any information (joint positions and so on) on to the fabric (wrong side) after you have cut it out and removed the pattern. Fold the fabric in half, selvedge to selvedge, and pin the pattern to the fabric with the grain line arrows running in the direction of the grain of the material.

Fitting the pattern pieces on to the material economically is rather like playing with a jig-saw puzzle. Position any pattern piece marked with 'fold' on to the fold of the fabric first. If using a fabric with a long fur, do not fold fabric. You will need to cut out the pieces twice. Use sharp pointed scissors and cut through the fabric backing only. Otherwise you may cut some of the pile and this may show on the right side of the finished seam. You may not need to buy fabric for the paws, pads and ears; try placing these pattern pieces onto any of the small off-cuts before discarding them.

Opposite: This group of adventurous bears likes to hide in the chest of drawers in the study.

POSITIONING EARS AND EYES

To mark the suggested positions for the ears and eyes, sew and knot a thread in their places, leaving the thread ends on the right side of the fabric. When you have assembled the teddy bear, you will easily find the positions again, by following the loose threads. These positions are only suggestions, however: to give the bear more personality and expression you may want to put the ears and eyes in different places. You make this choice when the bear is assembled.

MAKING THE HOLES FOR THE JOINTS

Before you start to assemble the bear, you must pierce the holes in the joint positions. This is much easier if done before the limbs are assembled. Using the awl (p.15), push a hole for the joint shanks on the marked positions of the arms, the legs and the back of the body.

STUFFING

The length and thickness of the fur can make a great deal of difference to the overall look of the bear. If you use a material that does not have a pile, you must take more care in stuffing and moulding, otherwise the bear could look lumpy. This applies to the paws and feet particularly. The thicker the material the smoother the finish and the more professional the look.

It is most important to use the correct amount of stuffing. Too little will make the bear look shapeless and it will not sit or stand properly; too much and it will look hard, not very cuddly and may strain the seams, which could burst.

EYES

In general, with bears, smaller eyes look better and impart more character than larger eyes. If in doubt, choose the smaller. Remember that 'safety-lock' eyes must be used if the bear is intended for a child, especially a child under three years old.

SEWING TIPS FOR TEDDY BEARS

- Set the sewing machine to the shortest straight stitch to sew the seams. This makes the stitching strong so the bear can stand up to years of enthusiastic play.
- Finish all seams properly. Reverse stitch (p.24) at the beginning and end of each seam, or tie off the threads very carefully. This will ensure that the seams will not unravel during rough treatment.
- Sew very slowly on the machine when sewing thick material. This will avoid either the needle or the thread breaking.
- Keep the machine well oiled, particularly when using fluffy fabrics.
- Always clip curved seam allowances carefully; this is important for giving the bear a smooth, round shape.
- Double-stitch tight corners and pressure points. These are the areas that could burst and come apart.
- If directed to 'ease' (p.19) while joining two seams, this requires you to stretch the shorter or smaller side, to fit.
- Buttonhole thread or dental floss can be used instead of six-stranded embroidery

Opposite: Clean feet and paws are essential if a furry bear is to become successful in a chosen career.

cotton (thread) when you require a strong thread for sewing in the eyes or attaching the head to the body.

- Keep your special hand-made bear in good repair. Mend any damage as soon as it appears.

GENERAL SEWING HINTS

- The thread that comes off the reel first is the end that should be put through the needle when hand sewing to prevent the thread knotting. In other words, never cut the thread until you have threaded the needle.
- To keep your needles and pins rust free, use raw wool (with natural lanolin) to stuff your pin cushion.
- When threading your needle, put something white, such as paper, behind the eye of the needle. This makes it easier to see the thread.
- When machine-sewing slippery fabrics, place tissue paper between the layers to keep them from slipping. After stitching, tear the paper away.
- To help keep your thimble in place, lick your finger before putting it on.
- Ironing felt is not necessary. If felt becomes wet it will shrink, so if it is necessary to press seams, use a dry iron.

STITCH GUIDE

Ladder stitch – This is a stitch used to bring two edges together invisibly. In the case of making a bear, use this stitch to sew up the openings left for the stuffing. Bring the needle through from behind at A. Insert the needle at B, then puch it along the fabric to bring it out at C. Insert at D. Continue in this way, pulling the thread tight until the two edges close neatly.

Whip stitch – This stitch is used to join two edges together. In making the bear, use this stitch to attach the ear to the head. Bring the needle from the back of the work in a diagonal way over the two surfaces to be joined, working in a forward direction.

Satin stitch – This stitch is used for filling in a space, as in the case of the bear's nose. Use a thick stranded cotton (thread) or a fine cord to give the stitch bulk. Use straight stitches worked closely together to give an even, padded effect. The stitches should be niether too long or too loose as they are liable to be pulled out of position.

Running stitch – This stitch is used to hold a hem or folded edge in place, particularly in a small difficult position where pinning is awkward. Insert the needle over and under the cloth, making small stitches of even length. This stitch can be pulled out when the final row of machine stitching is complete.

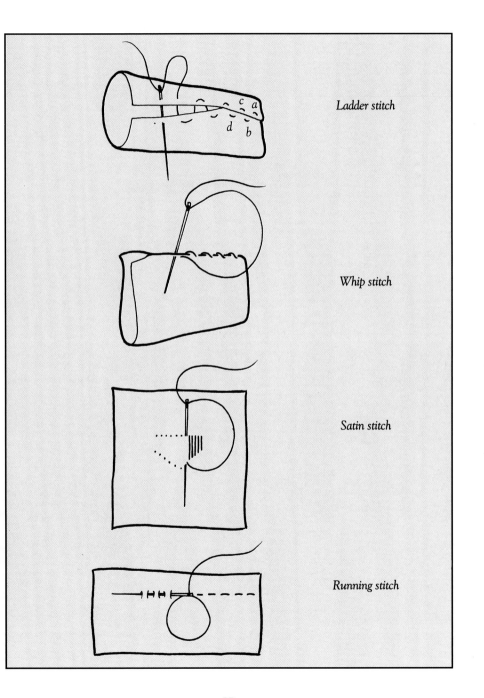

Ladder stitch

Whip stitch

Satin stitch

Running stitch

FINISHING TECHNIQUES

ONE OF THE MORE enjoyable aspects of making your teddy bear has to be deciding what he or she should wear. In fact, all they need to wear apart from their own natural 'coat' is a ribbon around their neck, or maybe a gold chain, an earring or a bracelet would be more appropriate.

Give careful thought to your choice of fabrics for making and dressing your bears. Contrast and co-ordinate your fabrics and colours and use old laces and braids to give an extra special look. There is no need to go to any great expense in dressing the bears. For a simple but feminine look, 30cm (12 inches) of old lace threaded on to a pretty piece of ribbon can be appealing.

Of course, the choice of outfits is endless. You could make a hand-knitted jumper embroidered with the bear's name (or, if it is to be a christening present, the child's name and date of birth); you could dress your bear in an outfit appropriate to the season. Doll's hats are available in many interesting styles and you are sure to find one to fit your bear. Bears are often used as mascots – why not knit the bear a scarf and hat in the owner's favourite team's colours – and bears in uniforms are always popular.

If your teddy bear is to be a gift, give some thought to the tastes and interests of the recipient, or maybe dress the teddy in an outfit appropriate to the occasion or celebration.

Maybe you would like to make a family of bears, Mother, Father and Baby. If so, you can enlarge the pattern (p.32) slightly for the Father, and make it a little smaller for the Baby. Do this by photocopying the pages of the book, then you will be able to cut out the pattern directly instead of tracing. It is most important that you enlarge all the pattern pieces at the same rate; likewise for the smaller size.

LABELS AND NAMES

You may wish to label your teddy bear with the teddy bear's name, the date of completion and your signature. Special woven fabric labels can be printed to your specific design or they can be purchased from a haberdashery store. If you intend to take up 'producing teddy bears' in a serious way, getting your own labels printed would be necessary.

The label should be filled in, folded in half end-to-end, then the rough edge should be sewn into one of the seams during construction. The most appropriate place is behind an arm or a leg, or between the legs in the centre-back seam. Ensure the label is not too big for the size of bear.

Opposite: Bears, like cats, like to play and hide in boxes.

BEGINNER'S PROJECT

THIS CHARMING and engaging character is an easy beginner's project. The fur fabric is soft and the pile is not too long so the sewing process is easier for those who have not previously made a bear. The paws and pads are of soft leather, but can be made of felt as an alternative. The limbs are jointed using a simple procedure and this gives a professional result to the bear.

MATERIALS
- 40cm x 144cm (16 x 56 inches) jersey-backed fur fabric.
- 25cm x 25cm (10 x 10 inches) approx. of soft leather or felt.
- Scrap of apricot satin for inner ears.
- 250 g (about 8 oz) polyester filling.
- 1 doll-maker's needle.
- 2 pairs (4 joints) 4.5cm (1¼ inches) teddy bear joints.
- 1 pair 12mm (½ inch) teddy bear eyes, or 2 boot buttons.
- 1 skein dark brown stranded embroidery cotton (thread) for nose.
- 1 reel sewing machine thread to match bear fabric.
- 1 skein stranded embroidery cotton (thread) to match bear fabric.
- 90cm (36 inches) ribbon for neck tie.
- Stuffing tool (such as a wooden-spoon handle or chop-stick).

Above: Some of the items necessary to make the project.

The pattern for the bear is printed actual size on the following nine pages. You need to photocopy it accurately. On pages 34 and 35, you need to photocopy the pieces and join them to make the pattern the correct size. Once you have photocopied and cut out the pattern pieces, follow the pattern guide on page 41. Note that the arrows on the pattern pieces indicate which way the pattern pieces are to be placed on the grain of the fabric.

Opposite: The completed project bear made in a fur fabric.

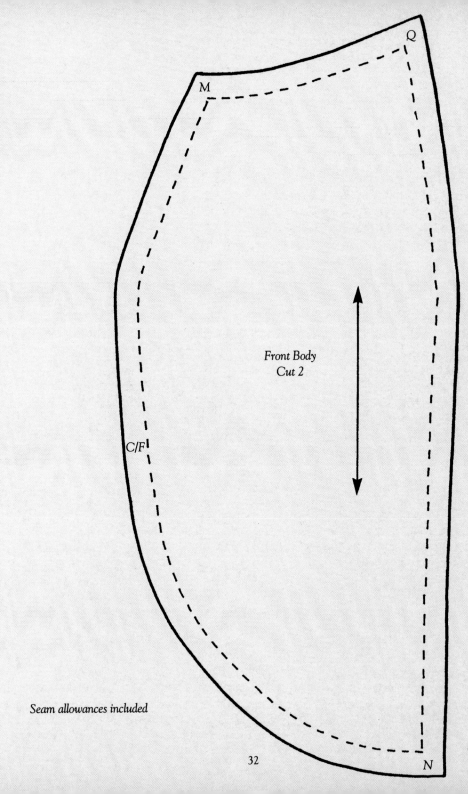

Q

M

Front Body
Cut 2

C/F

Seam allowances included

32

N

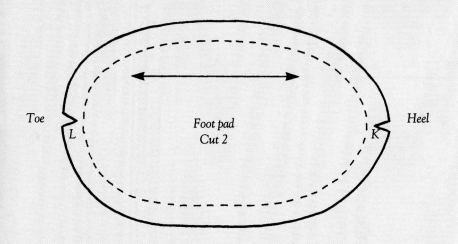

Toe

Heel

Foot pad
Cut 2

L

K

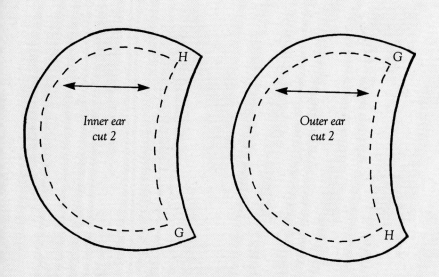

H

Inner ear
cut 2

G

G

Outer ear
cut 2

H

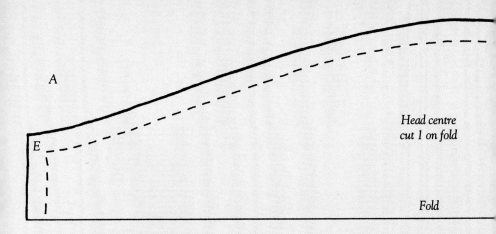

A

E

Head centre
cut 1 on fold

Fold

When you photocopy these two pages, press the gutter down as flat as possible to ensure you copy the inner edge of the pattern pieces. Make sure you join the pieces with tape accurately, so that A measures 26.5cm (10½ inches) and B measures 18cm (7 inches) from P to Q.

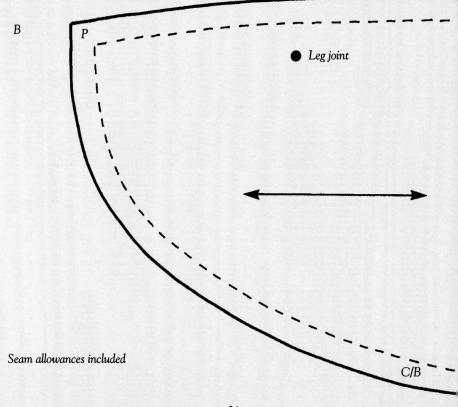

B

P

● Leg joint

Seam allowances included

C/B

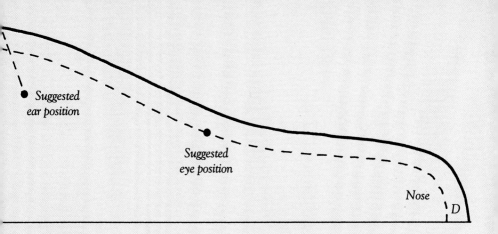

Suggested
ear position

Suggested
eye position

Nose

D

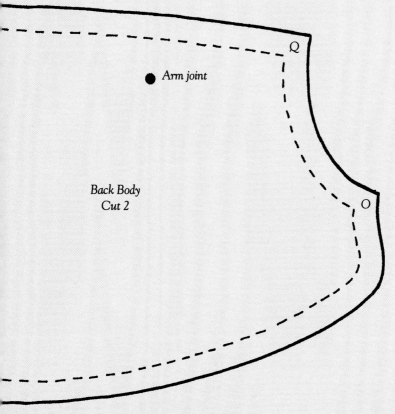

Arm joint

Back Body
Cut 2

Q

O

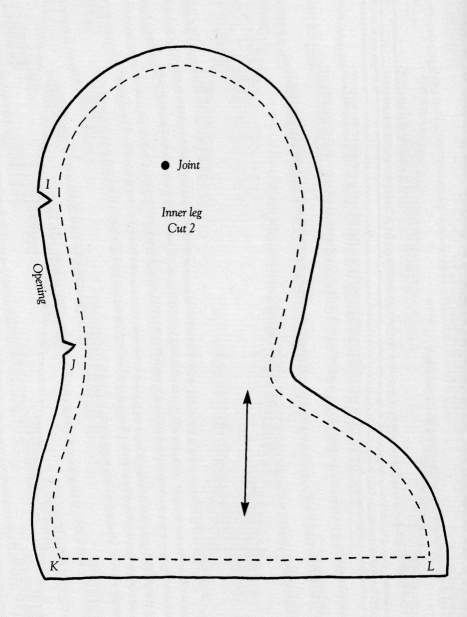

Joint

Inner leg
Cut 2

I

Opening

J

K

L

Seam allowances included

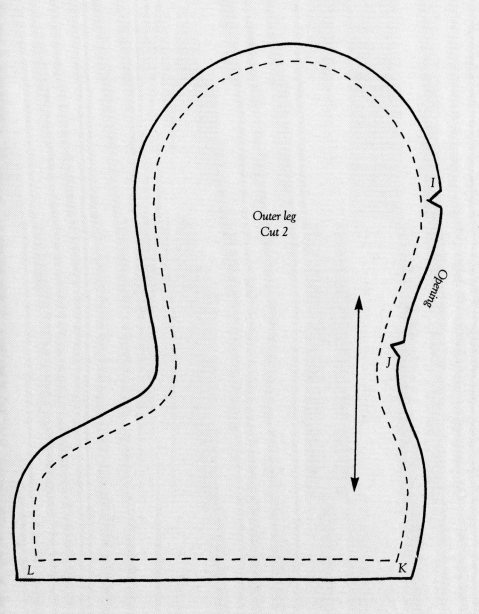

Outer leg
Cut 2

I

Opening

J

L

K

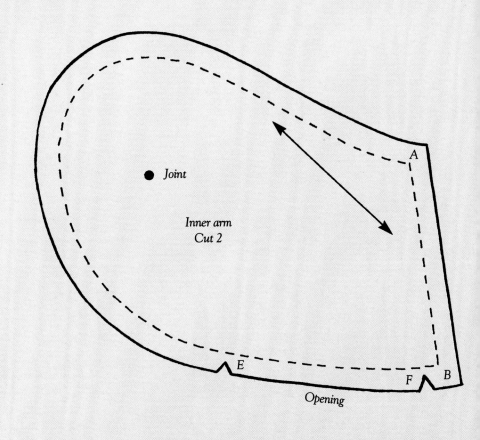

Joint

Inner arm
Cut 2

E

F

B

Opening

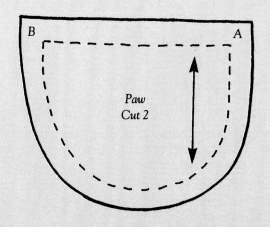

B

A

Paw
Cut 2

Seam allowances included

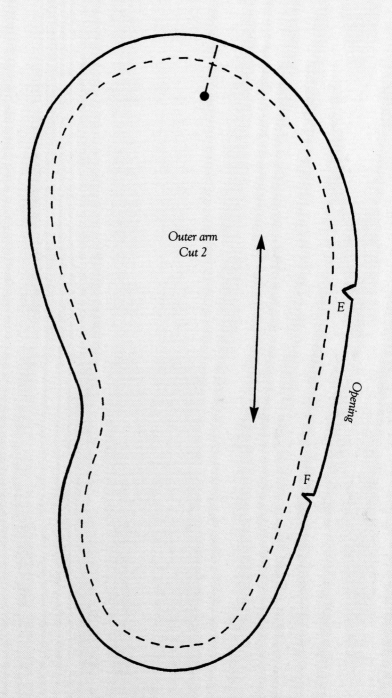

Outer arm
Cut 2

E

F

Opening

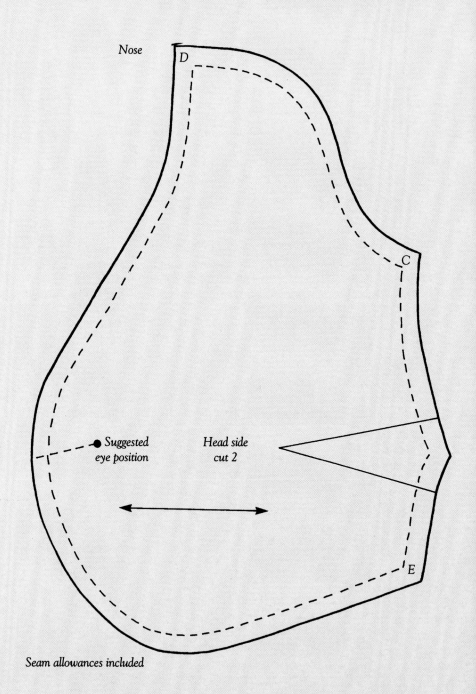

Nose

D

C

● Suggested
eye position

Head side
cut 2

E

Seam allowances included

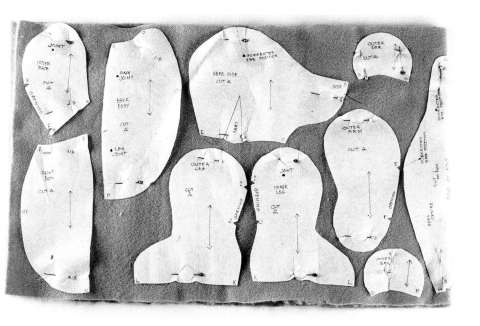

Above: Lay out the pattern pieces for the bear on the wrong side of the fabric as shown
Below: Cut carefully (with sharp scissors) around the pattern pieces through the double thickness.

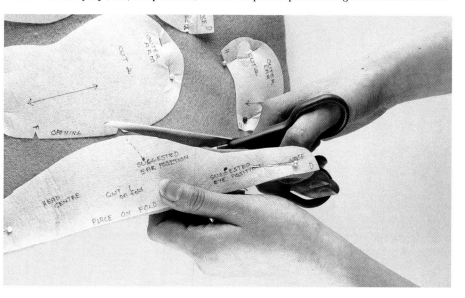

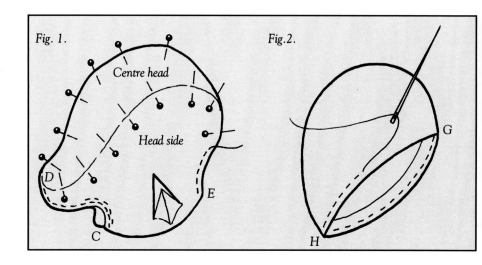

Step One: The Head (Fig. 1)

Pin and sew darts on head sides. Pin and sew together seam from D (nose) to C (neck). Double stitch at curve of neck. Clip curved seam allowance. Pin the head centre in between the head sides. Sew from E (neck) to D (nose) then back to E (neck).

Take care sewing at the nose. Turn head to right-side out and put aside.

Step Two: The Ears (Fig. 2)

Pin left inner ear to left outer ear. Sew from G around to H. Ease as you sew, because the inner ear is slightly smaller than the outer ear. Turn ear right-side out. Press seam allowance and tack (baste). Place to one side. Repeat for right ear.

Step Three: The Arms (Fig. 3)

Pin leather paw to left inner arm. Sew from A to B and press seam open. Pin the inner arm to the left outer arm. Ease as you sew inner and outer together as the inner arm is slightly smaller than the outer arm. Leave an opening for stuffing between E and F. Clip curved allowances. Turn right-side out and place to one side. Repeat for right arm.

Step Four: The Legs (Fig. 4)

Pin left inner leg to left outer leg. Ease as you sew as inner leg is slightly smaller than outer leg. Sew leg together from L (toe) to K (heel) leaving an opening for stuffing between I and J. Pin L (toe) to foot pad to L (toe) on leg, K (heel) on foot pad to K (heel) on leg. Sew all the way round, easing a little. Clip curved seam allowance on front of leg. Turn right-side out and place to one side. Repeat for the right leg.

Step Five: The Body

Pin and sew centre back from O (neck) to P (groin). Pin and sew centre front from M (neck) to N (groin). Pin and sew front body onto back body from Q (neck) down, joining groin, then sew up to Q (neck). Turn body

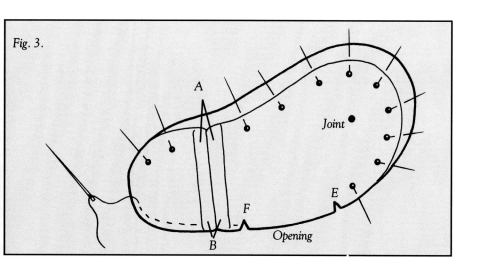

Fig. 3.

right-side out and place to one side.

Step Six: Stuffing the Head

Begin by pushing very small pieces of stuffing into the nose. Continue using reasonably small pieces which helps to give a smooth finish to the shape. When stuffing the head, you need to mould the shape in your hands; this helps to create the difference in the look of each bear. Squeeze, rub and knead the head until you have a balanced, firmly-stuffed head. Place to one side.

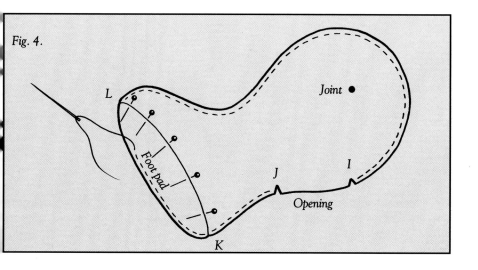

Fig. 4.

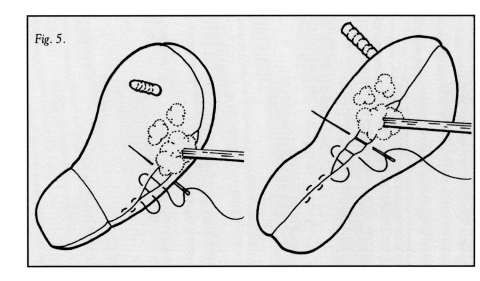

Fig. 5.

Step Seven: Stuffing the Legs and Arms (Fig. 5)

Begin by fitting the joint into place. Push the part of the joint which has the shank through the hole in the joint position – the disc is inside the limb, the shank comes through to the outside. Stuff the paws and toes as for the head, pressing in the small pieces firmly using a stuffing tool like a wooden-spoon handle or chop stick: the success of this process makes the difference when a well-made bear and a badly-made bear. Continue stuffing the limbs firmly, then close the openings using ladder stitch (p.26) with a needle and matching thread.

Step Eight: Joining the Legs and Arms to the Body

Pay special attention to placing the limbs in the right direction – facing forward. Once you have snapped the joints in place, they cannot be taken apart.

Push the joint shank of the limb through the appropriate joint position to the inside of the body, place on washer, then snap on fastening disc. Snap together as far and as tight as possible.

Step Nine: Stuffing the Body

Stuff the body as you did the rest of the bear. Pay special attention to the hump and around the shanks of the limbs. Mould the shape and stuff firmly.

Step Ten: Attaching the Head

Tack (baste), using a thread to match the fur fabric, around the neck openings of both head and body. Ease a little as you sew. Secure the thread. Place head in position on top of body, nose facing forward. Stitch in place where front and back seams of the head meet with front and back seams of the body. Secure firmly. Thread a doll-maker's needle with strong matching thread. Sew around the neck

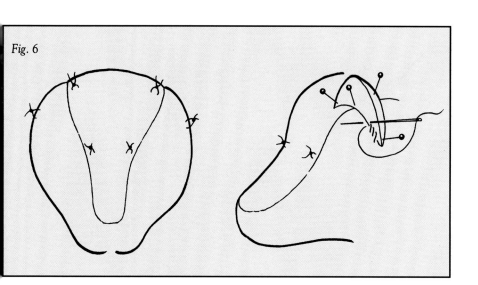

Fig. 6

with firm stitches, several times. Finishing stitches securely. This is a weak point in the bear's construction, so you may like to use fabric glue at this point after the first round of securing stitches.

Step Eleven: Attaching the Ears (Fig. 6)
Pin left and right ear on either side of the head. Stitch with matching thread, using whip stitch (p.26). Secure well as bears are frequently picked up by the ears.

Step Twelve: Sewing in the Eyes (Fig.7)
Using a doll-maker's needle, secure the thread at left eye position, thread needle through button or eye shank; push needle through left eye position, come out at right eye position and thread needle through second button or eye shank. Bring the needle back through right eye position to left eye position. Do this several time, catching the shanks each time and pulling the stitching

tight as you go. This is an important part of the process which gives the bear its unique expression and personality.

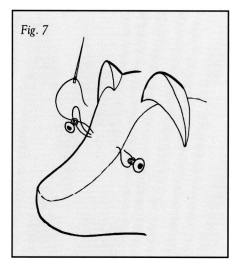

Fig. 7

Step Thirteen: The Nose (Fig. 8)

Use six strands of the nose-colour embroidery cotton (thread) and follow the steps illustrated. Using satin stitch (p.26) fill in the triangle of the nose in the position indicated in (a). When finished, bring the needle out at the bottom centre of the nose. Push needle through and out of the indicated spot in (b). Loop needle around the thread from the base of the nose to the left-hand spot, then push the needle up through the top centre spot as shown in (c). Finish securely in amongst the satin stitching (p.26) of the nose.

Congratulations, you have completed your first hand-made teddy bear. Tie a ribbon or bow around his neck and start planning your next project.

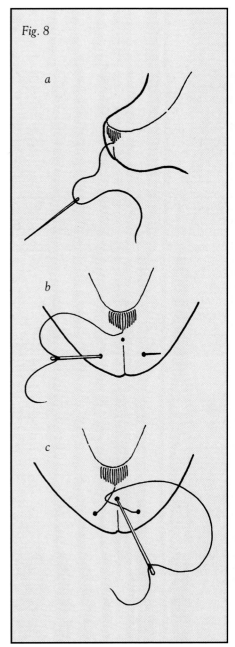

Fig. 8

a

b

c

INDEX